Each Inner Workbook is a self-study retreat or workshop that you can do at home. They are designed to become a part of your day, just like that first cup of tea, and invite you to journal the experience as you develop your practice, making it your own.

Contents

Introduction

We are each the living expression of our purpose, an embodiment of our reason for being. The life you have chosen, on this planet, in this beautiful body at this precise time is an articulation of your purpose.

Everything your mind wants to know about your purpose is already known to your soul, and this workbook is simply a guide, a doorway into what you already know to be true. Your essence contains the blueprint, and if you are patient, everything will be revealed over time.

In reality, it is possible to live a meaningful and fulfilling life without ever defining your purpose. Many do. Your innate ability to feel joy, express love and connect to meaning is always there. However, for some, and perhaps for you as you have chosen this workbook, it feels important, essential even, to find words to describe your purpose and to feel connected to your purpose. That in articulating purpose, you can feel a sense of wholeness and understand who you are and why you are here. This is really a case of your mind wanting to catch up with what your soul already knows.

If by the end of this workbook you haven't found the answer to your question, don't worry; these matters cannot be rushed or forced simply to satisfy the mind. Trust and have faith that you will find what you are seeking, even if it comes long after you have completed these pages – it will come and everything you do in this workbook will have played a part in your ultimate discovery.

With that in mind, this workbook has been written as a guide, a set of questions, exercises and experiments designed to open your heart and allow your inner intuition to rise from within. At times, your mind may be frustrated that there are no clear answers to your questions. For this reason, there are exercises to help you pause and settle your mind along the way.

As you embark on this journey, know that the answers to your deepest questions cannot be fuelled by desire, comparison or guilt. Know that your purpose cannot be copied by another, which in turn means you also cannot copy another person's purpose.

This would feel the opposite of purpose – empty, lacklustre and unfulfilling. Instead, the answers to your deepest questions will rise up from within in the same way water finds its way to the surface, breaks through the Earth's crust, becomes a gentle spring that leads to a stream, that becomes a river and eventually makes its way to the ocean. This is the place you are accessing inside yourself. The vast, borderless ocean within.

Be patient, take your time, and let go of any need to answer the question at all. Instead, can you simply enjoy the journey and all the goodness that makes this your extraordinary, precious life?

How to use
this workbook

I have recorded each of the
meditations included in the
workbook for you to listen to.

https://innerworkproject.com/
product/on-purpose/

There are two ways to use this workbook. Firstly, there will be the time you spend reading and answering the questions. Unlike an exam paper where there is a right answer, this is a reflective practice, meaning that as you write, you will often feel incomplete with no answers emerging, which can feel frustrating. In fact, as you unravel the different threads of your consciousness, you might find more questions than answers. Stick with it, as the not knowing, the frustration and having more questions than answers are all normal. It's a sign that you are doing the inner work, so take your time and know that there is no rush to reach an answer. On this occasion, being slow is best.

If you are experienced in personal growth and reflective practice, this is an opportunity to go deeper. As you write, let go of what you already know and consider the paths less travelled, the hidden corners of your being that may hold the keys to understanding your unique essence.

The second way to use this workbook is the space between.

Time away from the workbook is as useful as time sitting with it. Whether you find sparks of inspiration walking in nature, or if your revelations come in dreams that whisper fragments of a forgotten past, be open to the signs that point towards your truth.

Embrace the constant threads and the evolving wisdom that accompanies you on your journey wherever it comes from. Remember to let things percolate. The answers will come in time, usually when you're least expecting it.

Trust in the process of reflection, knowing that inner work and the quest for self-discovery is not a destination but a continual unfolding as you keep delving into the mysteries of your own being.

What is purpose

On Purpose

The reason identifying purpose feels so big is that you are attempting to define your reason for existence. Phew. Take a moment and take a breath – that is a lot! It is helpful to relax and know that your existence is the reason for your existence.

That you are here is enough.

When you find the words that define your purpose, it's likely to be only one or two words. Often people are surprised at how obvious and simple it is when they finally connect to the language of their purpose. They usually say: 'Is that it?!' This is because we confuse purpose with something we are here to do – big or small. Whereas purpose is an expression of your inner being. Of who you are, not what you do.

Therefore, it's okay if you don't find the words to articulate your purpose in four weeks. This can take a long time to understand, but in the meantime know that you are already fulfilling your purpose simply by being here.

What it is not?

Since the essence of purpose, the reason for existing, is such a significant question, people often shift the true meaning of purpose into an objective, result or outcome. Something to be accomplished or achieved. This is not wrong; we require a sense of purpose or a deliberate intention to accomplish things. Other times when people feel stuck in a rut or directionless they want to find a plan to help them get out and to create movement. This plan may be driven by purpose, but it's important to remember that a plan is not your purpose. To help differentiate these different places we can use the phrases opposite.

People can get confused and believe that their Core Purpose will help them understand what they should do with their life, almost as though knowing their Core Purpose will show them what career path they should follow. These are equally important questions, and sometimes connecting to Core Purpose makes these questions easier to answer. But for now, our focus in this workbook will be in helping you to articulate your Core Purpose.

People often get stuck with purpose because they think it should be something huge, something that will really make a meaningful difference to the world. This becomes too daunting and so the question is

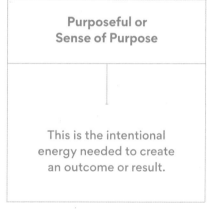

Core Purpose

This is your life purpose, the definition of who you are and why you are here.

Purposeful or Sense of Purpose

This is the intentional energy needed to create an outcome or result.

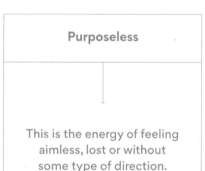

Purposeless

This is the energy of feeling aimless, lost or without some type of direction.

avoided altogether. One of the wonderful freedoms that comes from disconnecting your Core Purpose from what you do for your work is that purpose then becomes really simple. Of course, often the work we do is an expression of our purpose, but it is not the only place we express purpose. This is a particular relief for people who don't love their job or who have found that fulfilment didn't come from their work in the way they thought it would. You are a living expression of your purpose: in the way that you relate to others, in your parenting, your relationships, your hobbies, and the way you love to spend your free time.

Even in your work purpose can show up in many forms. For example, my purpose is *'To Heal'*. This is expressed in many ways, including but not limited to: writing, coaching, sound healing, speaking and teaching. This means my work as an Executive Coach is an expression of my purpose, as much as being an Author or Sound Healer is. In coaching, I know people have connected to their purpose when they can describe it in two words. For most people the idea that purpose can be distilled down to two words is hard to believe, but with over twenty years' experience of coaching leaders in business, this is my ultimate litmus test for purpose! The other test is that

purpose is equally for yourself as it is for others. Don't worry about doing that for yourself at this stage. Instead, relax as we explore some examples of Core Purpose.

I met a woman who was a living expression of her purpose. Her face beamed liked the sun as she walked me around her vegetable garden, explaining how she had learned how to plant biodynamically in tune with the rhythms of nature and without pesticides. Her purpose, it seemed to me, is *'To Grow'* and while she is a gardener, she could also have been a football coach who grew talent, or an apothecary who grew herbs for remedies, or a banker who grew money.

I asked a client the big question: 'Why are you here?' and he answered: 'I'm here to build things.' His purpose is clearly *'To Build'*. This simple articulation can have may forms of expression. For instance, he may want to build strong values in his children, he may want to build a team of people who deliver projects, he might want to build a multi-million-pound building or bridge. Or perhaps he would feel contented simply building a garden shed! And in a book I read about the Sufi mystic Rumi, his purpose, it seemed to me, was *'To Love'*. This expression of his purpose showed up in his teachings, his poetry, his spiritual practice and his dance.

What is your relationship to purpose?

Before you dive into reconnecting to your Core Purpose, let's begin by exploring your relationship with purpose.

Sitting comfortably, place your right hand on your belly and gently rest your left hand over your right.

In your own time take two or three slow breaths, noticing the gentle rise and fall of your belly, and feel yourself settle.

With every breath bring your focus and attention to the core of you, so that you feel grounded and centred. Now ask yourself the questions listed here.

Write as much or as little as you want in response to these questions one by one. These are big questions, and if you need to come back to them one at a time, that's okay.

There's no need to answer them all at once unless you are ready. Sometimes, you will need to pause, reflect and integrate a previous answer before you can move on.

That is completely normal and a very healthy way to approach this inner work.

Ask yourself:

1. What do you imagine life is like for people who fulfil their purpose?

2. In discovering your purpose, how do you imagine life will be different?

3. Is it possible to live a good life without articulating purpose?

4. How satisfied could you be in life without knowing your purpose?

5. What does it feel like to be disconnected from purpose?

6. Can purpose change over time?

Who

'You're trailing a bright pathway
that you don't even know about'

Donna Ashworth, You

I?

Am

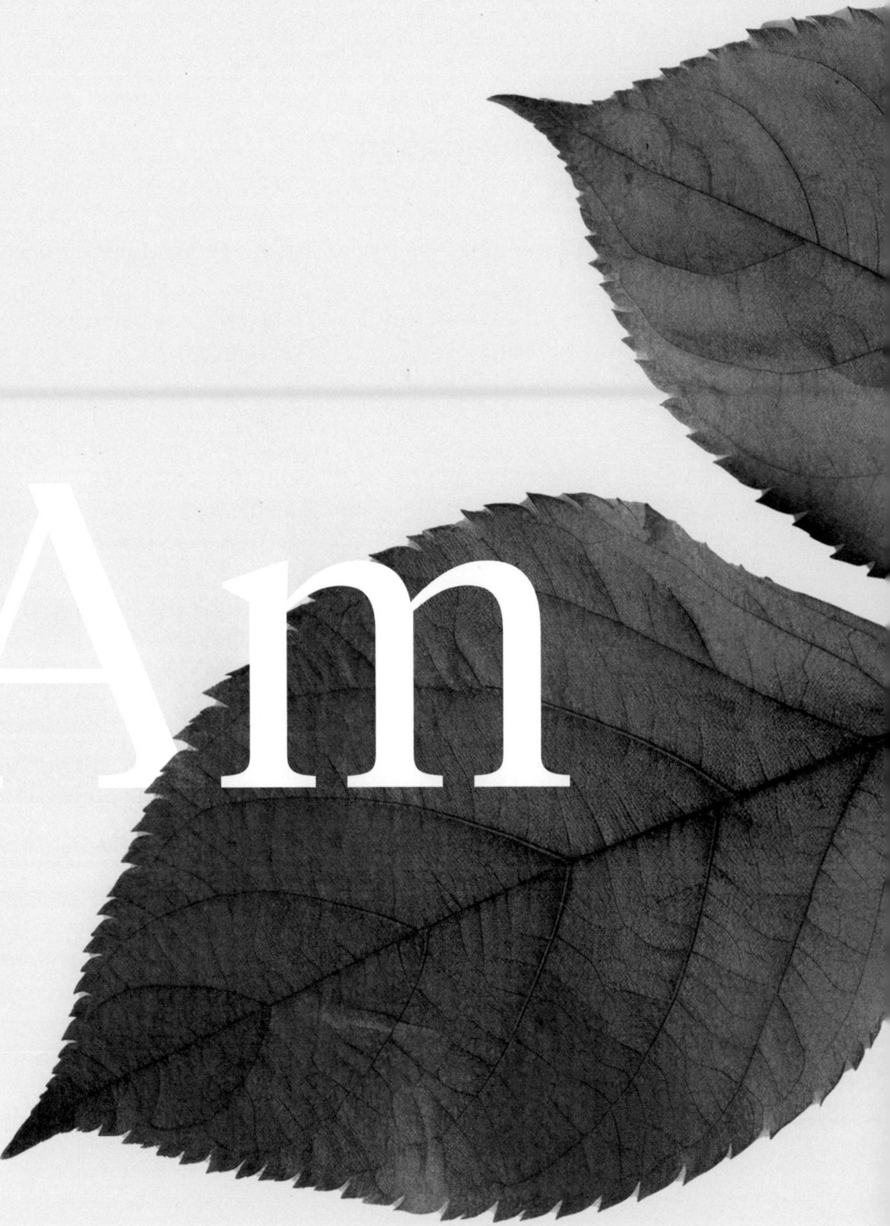

Week 1 Who Am I?

Day 1
Meditation: A conversation with your heart

Sit comfortably and place your right hand over your heart and your left hand over your right. Tip your chin down towards your chest, hunching forwards a little so that your chin is close to your hands.

Begin to feel the rhythm of your heartbeat beneath your hands. Gently cocooning yourself in this beautiful, life-sustaining rhythm. Slow your breathing down a little and let any tension or holding in your tummy start to soften, release and relax.

Now say your name silently to yourself and tell yourself all the things you appreciate about you. Whisper to your heart all that you are grateful for and let yourself know that you are loved, just as you are.

Now ask your heart what it would most like you to know about you at this time. Listen gently and let your heart whisper to you, knowing that your heart will talk with compassionate honesty and quiet courage.

When you are finished, return to a seated position and re-centre yourself with two or three intentional breaths, in through the nose and out through the mouth.

Beautiful – just like that. You are now ready to write.

Who am I?
You are going to practise some free-form writing, answering the same question several times, without censoring your answers, to allow yourself to fall deeper into your answers. Write from your heart, and if the words don't make sense, don't worry. Just continue to write and trust the process. Remember this is just the beginning; there is no need to get to an answer today.

Who am I?

I am...
I am...
I am...
I am...
I am...
I am...

Week 1 Who Am I?

Day 2
Clearing the way

Start by gathering some pencils, coloured pens or crayons – whatever you have to hand. Once you have what you need, get yourself settled in a relaxed seated position.

Close your eyes. Using your breath, begin to clear your mind. Imagine with every inhalation, a beautiful, cool, crisp, clearing sensation travelling in through your nose, up into the space between your eyebrows, and continuing to travel over the front of your brain. It's as if you are breathing in pure mountain air, as fresh snow falls on a winter's day.

As you breathe this cool, crisp, pure air, you feel it cleansing your mind. As you exhale, let any worries or concerns be released on the out breath. Breathing in pure, clear air, breathing out any worries or concerns. Letting your mind slow down and relax at a pace that is comfortable for you.

As you relax your mind, ask yourself: 'Who am I?' again. Today you are going to look for a response in the form of an image in your mind's eye. Rather than thinking or reasoning, simply let an image emerge.

Bring the image into your mind, letting it get sharper and clearer. Perhaps you hear something instead of seeing it. Or maybe you feel something; that's all welcomed. Let the process unfold naturally as it is intended for you.

When you are ready, open your eyes and write or draw what you saw in as much detail as possible. Include any feelings you had about the image and what it meant to you.

Space to create

Week 1 Who Am I?

Day 3
Higher source

The invitation today is to go outdoors for a walk. This walk is best taken in silence without other distractions. If you have a favourite crystal, put this in your pocket and then go for a walk, preferably in nature. As you walk, and when the moment feels right, ask again 'Who am I?' This time, let the response come through movement in your body. Trust its wisdom and let the movement unfold until you sense a completion.

Now, find a tree and sit at the base with your crystal. Absorb the goodness of who you are and the goodness that nature feeds you. Ask yourself again: 'Who am I?' This is an opportunity to ask for higher help. You are not alone.

When you return, write or draw about your experience.

" "

Not until we are lost do we begin to understand ourselves.

Henry David Thoreau

Space to create

Week 1 Who Am I?

Day 4
Unravelling identity

Sometimes parts of our personality or character are developed out of who we decide we don't want to be. More often than not, this is an aspect of a parent that had a big impact on us, and the mind responds by deciding to be less like them. For instance, if you had a father who was domineering you might want to be perceived as relaxed and easy-going. If your mother was often ill, you might want to be seen as strong.

It's not always a parent that influences these changes. It can also be a friend, a teacher or another close relative, and often these subtle shifts to our natural place are made from a mixture of people and experiences. When this happens, over time, you believe the narrative that this is now who you really are. In fact, to the outside world it seems like this is who you are; however, it is really a cover. Usually, this aspect resides in you naturally, but in the decision to be different it becomes overamplified as you attempt not to be a particular type of person. So, the question today will need you to take a deep breath and dive deep. Today the question is:

Who did you not want to be?

" "
I want to unfold.
Rainer Maria Rilke

Who did you not want to be?

Week 1 Who Am I?

Day 5
Connecting the dots

Today is an opportunity to draw out themes from the first four days. To do that, you can draw a mind map, a quick, visual tool that is useful when looking for themes and patterns. A mind map begins with a central question or idea, which you place in a bubble in the middle of the page. From the centre you can branch out your thoughts and ideas with more bubbles.

As this process is not linear, it allows you to access different parts of your brain and intuition. At first the process might seem random, but stay with it, and once you step back at the end, it will be possible to see the themes and patterns more clearly.

Begin your mind map with 'I am' in the middle. Branch off some key thoughts from the previous three exercises, then, as you build the mind map, start to group together any repeating themes as you notice them.

Begin to look at the page with soft eyes. Softening your gaze and your focus.

What do you start to observe about who you are. What do you see?

Write in one sentence: **I am...**

66 99
Do your work.
Then step back.

Lao Tzu

I am

Week 1 Who Am I?

Day 6
What do I most love?

We all have people, places and animals that we love, and while you can begin with these, this exercise is an opportunity to go beyond the external things you love and to ask your inner heart: 'What do I most love?' Imagine writing a poetic reply to this question: write about what moves you, what you yearn for, what your soul desires.
This is a time to express yourself and to be fuelled by the fire of passion and the steadiness of a timeless, unwavering love.

From the bottom of my heart, I most love...

What did you discover? What themes were there?

" "

Remember that wherever your heart is, there you will find your treasure.

Paulo Coelho, The Alchemist

From the bottom of my heart, I most love...

Week 1 Who Am I?

Day 7
Memory box

Now that you are clear on what you most love, it's time to consider what you might have lost along the way that you want to reclaim. Children often innately know what they love and gravitate towards it. When confidence gets knocked, or as responsibilities grow over time, the things you loved so much are slowly forgotten. Let's see what you can find by opening your memory box from the past.

66 99

Only a child sees things with perfect clarity, because it hasn't developed all those filters which prevent us from seeing things that we don't expect to see.

Douglas Adams

My memory box

My favourite **film** was:

My favourite **story** was:

The **book** I read again and again was:

I **fell** out of love with:

I really **miss**:

I went to school and **stopped**:

I **wish** I still:

I **long** for the times I used to:

I used to hear people tell me I was **good** at:

Week 2

Life

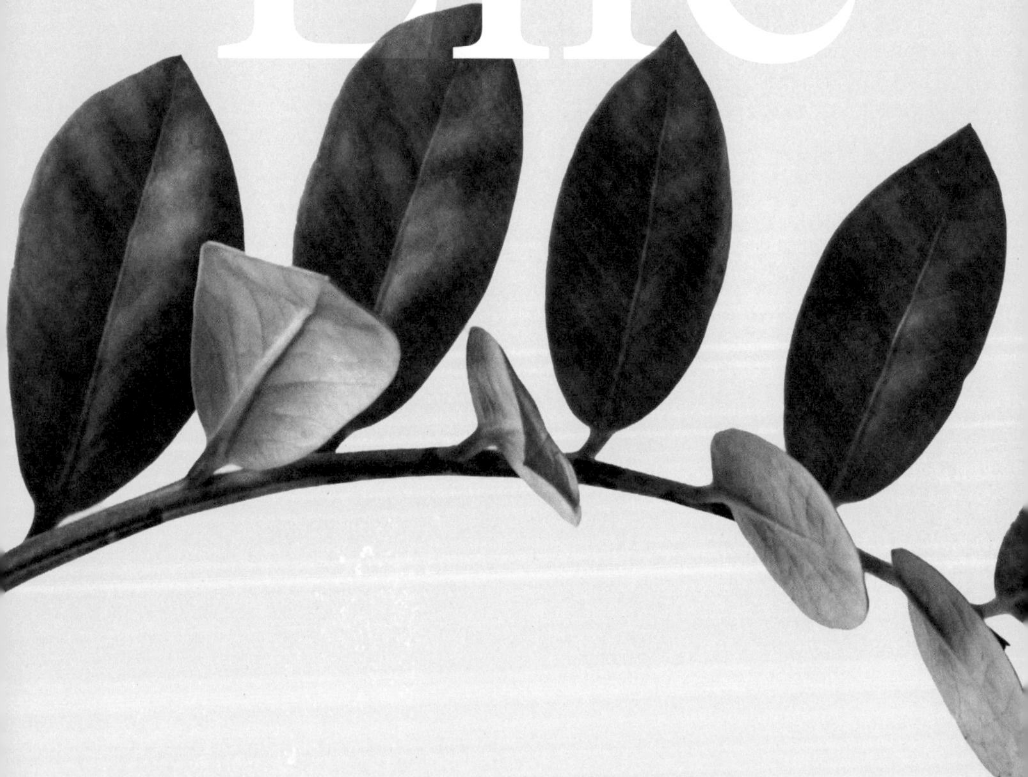

'On this path let the
          heart be your guide'

RUMI

Path

Week 2 Life Path

Finding the patterns
in your path

Your Life Path is an ever-unfolding journey, a series of events and experiences – moments past, present and future that are linked together, consisting of where you have come from, where you are now, and where you are going. Destination unknown. Running through these experiences is the essence of you, guiding you on your Life Path.

Often emphasis is placed on the future, and how to manifest and bring your desired future into being, but when we want to dive deeper into our purpose, it helps to pause, still the desire to move forwards and begin by looking backwards.

Approaching purpose in this way provides an opportunity to distill the experience of your life so far, to look for patterns in the path that can be clues to your purpose.

As you go about gathering nuts, you benefit from understanding yourself even more and begin to identify insights that can help you to become clearer about your purpose.

Sometimes we can be hesitant to look backwards. Our minds become protective and don't want us to revisit the old, painful times. We prefer not to open Pandora's Box and reveal the hidden hurts that we have locked away for a long time. This is understandable, but you can choose what you look back on, remembering that your triumphs and successes will be just as important here as you search for the hidden gems and your natural talents, and discover the beautiful impact of your gifts. Ultimately you are looking back to help you articulate your purpose, and in doing this you may discover a new level of integration and a sense of wholeness that you didn't even know had been missing.

For today, have a gentle look through your journalling so far and make a note of any words that particularly stand out or resonate with you.

Note to self

Week 2 Life Path

Reflection exercise:
Life Path

This is a key part of this week's inner work, so while it may seem daunting at first, it's worth taking your time with this exercise as it will give you a firm foundation and make the rest of the week flow with ease.

The aim is to look at each decade of your life and to recall the major milestones. For instance, even though you may not remember it, your first decade would include being born, going to school and forming new friendships. Perhaps siblings arrived, maybe you moved house, or other life events might have happened such as a divorce or a death in the family.

As you are looking back over several decades in this exercise, look for the headlines and key events, rather than going into lots of details; otherwise it will be exhausting.

If you want to stretch this exercise over a few days, that's okay, or you can come back to it over time. Remember, you are looking for the headlines rather than lots of detail. Starting with where you were living is a good route into the reflective process here.

Decade 1 From – To

Where did I live?

What were the major milestones?

What was the biggest challenge?

What went well?

Decade 2 From – To

Where did I live?

What were the major milestones?

What was the biggest challenge?

What went well?

Decade 3 From – To

Where did I live?

What were the major milestones?

What was the biggest challenge?

What went well?

Decade 4 From – To

Where did I live?

What were the major milestones?

What was the biggest challenge?

What went well?

Decade 5 From – To

Where did I live?

What were the major milestones?

What was the biggest challenge?

What went well?

Decade 6 From – To

Where did I live?

What were the major milestones?

What was the biggest challenge?

What went well?

Decade 7 From – To

Where did I live?

What were the major milestones?

What was the biggest challenge?

What went well?

Decade 8 From – To

Where did I live?

What were the major milestones?

What was the biggest challenge?

What went well?

Week 2 Life Path

Day 10
Meditation: A conversation with your intuition

In the previous exercise you were working with your left brain, sequencing facts, drawing on logic and using linear thinking. To balance this out, today you are going to take that set of linear information and view it using the right brain, which is the seat of your imagination, creativity and intuition.

Sit comfortably, with your spine straight, and allow your shoulders to relax. Close your eyes and keep your chin level with the floor. Take a breath in through your nose and exhale easily through an open mouth. Repeat three times, letting your belly soften with every exhale.

Place your attention on the space between your eyebrows. Now, imagine a beautiful, indigo light about one centimetre in front of this point. This deep blue-violet light hovers gently in the air, and when you are ready, you begin to let this light gently enter the space between your eyebrows.

You feel this healing light gently expanding and pulsating as you continue to breathe steadily. The powerful, healing, indigo light radiates and soothes as it expands beneath the surface of your forehead. As the light expands, you maintain your focus on the space between your eyebrows.

Now, with your focus on the space between your eyebrows, you ask your intuition what it would most like you to know about you at this time. Give space for the response to come in any form: a colour, a memory, a feeling, an image, a sound, a smell. Trust whatever comes to you, knowing this is your intuition speaking.

Finally, let the indigo light soothe your entire body and mind, sending the light to any parts of you that might need it the most at this time.

When you are finished, re-centre yourself with two or three intentional breaths, in through the nose and out through the mouth, and slowly open your eyes.

The next step is to write or draw the key milestones on your Life Path on the following pages. Start wherever you want and let your intuition guide you. Express your story in the way that feels right to you. Have fun, play, and enjoy yourself!

My Life Path

Week 2 Life Path

Day 11
Finding the gifts

Looking back at the Life Path you completed yesterday, consider the following questions:

- Where in your life was the path easy?

- Where in your life did the path feel smooth?

- Where has there been beauty along the way?

- Where were the moments that most moved you?

Now bring everything together by writing a short letter to yourself about your life so far. In your letter, write to yourself as though you were writing to your best friend.

Describe what and who you have loved, what you have most enjoyed. Write about the moments where you felt you really thrived. What did you find easy? When did you feel most alive?

Look for the good stuff.
Find the treasures.

Discover the gold

Space to create

Week 2 Life Path

Day 12
The chapters of your story

You are going to keep exploring the Life Path that you completed a few days ago. Today, you will use movement to support your reflective process, by going for a walk. This walk is best completed without distractions, so, if possible, leave your devices at home, disconnecting from technology so that you can connect more deeply with yourself. As you walk, reflect on the Life Path exercise from Day 10 and consider the chapters of your own story. For ease, the suggestion would be for you to identify four distinct chapters. For example, the chapters could be:

- Childhood, fun and friendship, parenting, career.

  or
- Growing up, sports achievements, university days, love lessons.

  or
- My family, places I lived, proudest accomplishments, where the impossible became possible.

  or
- Younger years, my big passion, giving back, later years.

What insights do these chapters give you about your purpose?

Unfold your myth

The chapters of my life

Week 2 Life Path

Day 13
A snapshot of your life

Now that you have had a chance to consider the chapters of life so far, it is time to find four photographs that tell your story. Obviously, your life is more than four photographs, but this is a beautiful way to celebrate the journey you have been on to this point in time. As you think about your life as a series of chapters so far, know that it is an unfolding life story with more yet to come.

Using the chapters you defined yesterday, find four photos, one for each chapter. Print them off and either stick them into the spaces in your workbook or you can frame them as a celebration of your life so far.

As you complete this exercise, reflect on any thoughts and feelings that arise.

66 99
Photography for me is not looking, it's feeling.
Don McCullin

Space to create

Week 2 Life Path

Day 14
Mind map exercise: Guiding compass

As this week's inner work draws to a close, let's use another mind map; this time to bring the threads of your reflections together. Using the points of the compass as your guide consider the following questions:

West: From your story, what is it time to let go of?

North: From your story, where have you faced difficulties and what did these teach you?

East: Based on your story so far, what would a good life look like for you now?

South: Knowing what you know now, how would you describe your purpose, your reason for being?

Feel into it.
Breathe into it.

Footnote: If any of the exercises this week have triggered something in your awareness and you need additional support, please do reach out to a relevant person in your support network.

N

W   E

S

Wis

'Listen to the wind, it talks.
Listen to the silence, it speaks.
Listen to your heart, it knows'

Native American proverb

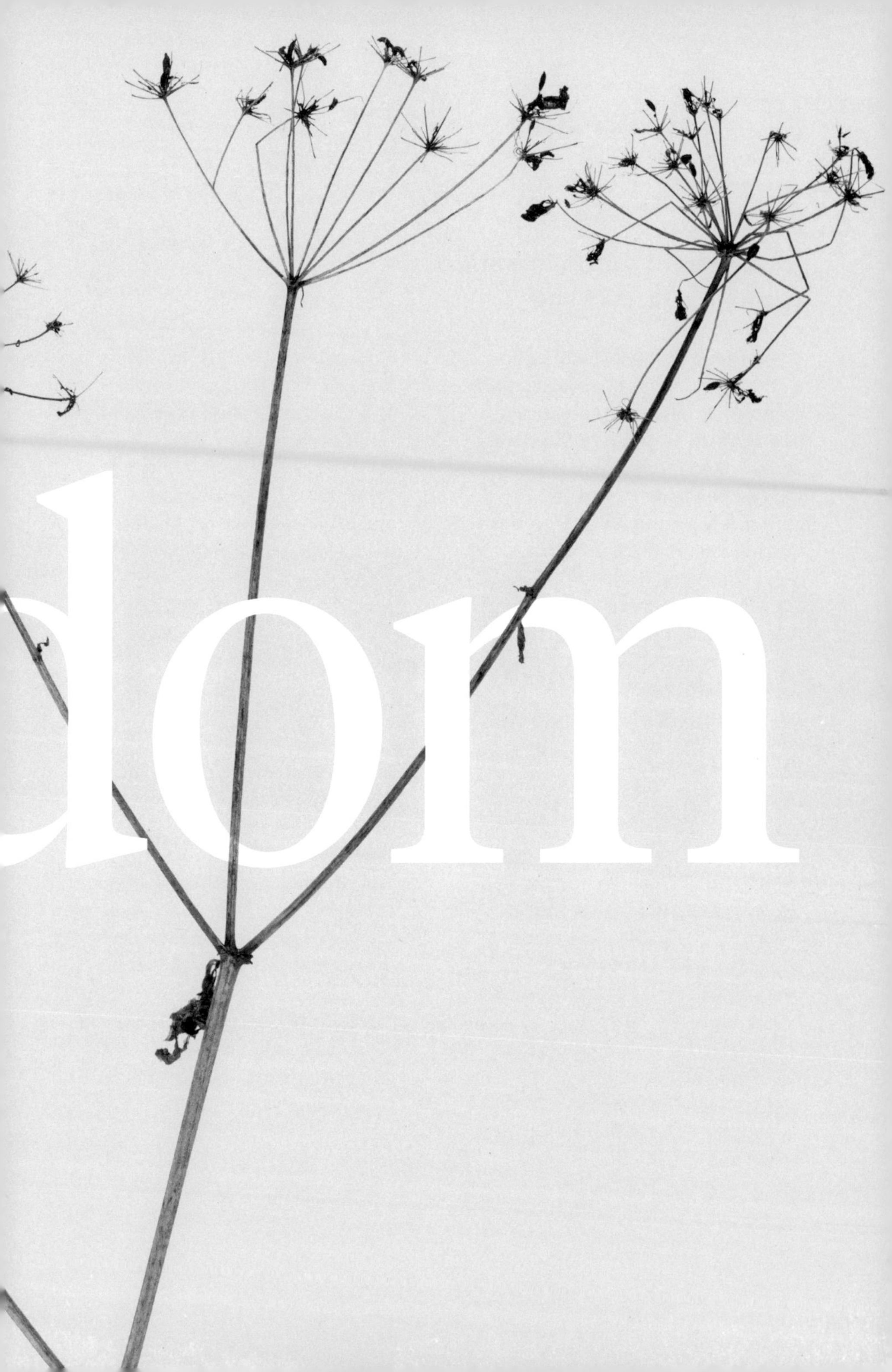
dom

Week 3 Wisdom

Day 15
Meditation: A conversation with your higher self

If you found last week's reflection a stretch, or even a challenge, that's completely natural. You were like a deep sea diver, going to the depths of your own inner ocean. You are now on the ascent, and, as with diving, it is a good time to go slowly. You have done the hard work.

Lay down on your back, somewhere that you can be comfortable for a few minutes. Support your body with pillows, blankets or bolsters, so you can relax deeply. Let your arms rest gently by your sides, palms facing upwards, and notice your feet softening as you begin to relax and let go.

Imagine you are laying on a beautiful, soft cloud. The cloud holds you and envelops you, so that you feel completely safe. As you lie on this soft cloud, you are aware of the earth beneath you and the expanse of sky above you.

On your next exhale, you notice that your body and mind feel as light as a feather – the edges of you soften and you feel like a cloud.

Soft and expansive, all the hard edges of you dissolve and melt away. You smile and feel grateful to simply be here.

From this place of softness and expansion, you say silently to yourself:

'Earth beneath me.
Sky above me.
Water within me.
Air around me.
I am okay.'

Breathe and repeat the affirmation two or three times.

Place your hand on your heart and connect again with the steady rhythm of your heartbeat. Begin to feel the edges of you making contact with the surface beneath you.

Wiggle your fingers and toes, then stretch and open your eyes. Take some time to arrive fully back in the room.

Who or what supports you in your daily life?

What helps you to feel safe and secure?

What are you grateful for?

Week 3 **Wisdom**

Day 16
Silver threads

Now that you have made contact with your higher self, today you are going to take that experience to another level.

Begin by placing your index and middle fingers at the point where your collarbones meet. Working from this centre point and moving out towards the shoulders, slowly rub your fingers along your collarbones to activate the energy in this area. You can also rub the area above and below the collarbones.

Now, resting your fingers on your collarbones, imagine there are beautiful strands of silver thread beneath your fingers. Using the power of your imagination, you are going to send those silver strands out from your body. Each thread will remain attached to you, but like a silver starburst they will also leave your body, sending out a pulse of energy. As you send out each thread, you will ask a question. Ask the questions one by one, sending out the threads and then seeing what pulses of energy return to you...

- What do I love?
- What do I find easy?
- When have I felt whole?
- When have I been magnetic?
- When have my gifts been received?
- What do I believe?
- What am I seeking?

Trust the process, take your time, and stay open to the messages, however they come to you.

When you have finished, draw each of the threads back in, one by one, letting them rest underneath your collarbones. Know that they are always there for you to access when you are seeking higher guidance.

Write your responses opposite.

Space to create

Big love to you, you're doing great!

Week 3 Wisdom

Day 17
Something special

Universal symbols are all around us, so much so we rarely notice them – for example:
- a heart symbolizes love,
- the oak tree symbolizes strength,
- a white dove symbolizes peace.

In your life, everyday objects will have taken on symbolism for you. For example, a robin may be a symbol for a loved one who has died, and so each time you see a robin you are reminded of that person. A wedding ring is a daily symbol of a lifelong promise you have made to yourself and your partner. Beyond physical objects, a personal symbol can also be something that you design yourself. This is today's exercise: to draw a personal symbol (real or imagined) that represents the essence of you. If you own the object, you may also want to reconnect with it and the meaning it gives to you.

This is an intuitive exercise, so let yourself be guided.

Trust the whispers from within.

66 99

For in the dew of little things the heart finds its morning and is refreshed.

Khalil Gibran

Space to create

Week 3 **Wisdom**

Day 18
Shine

> 'Nothing can dim the light that shines from within.'
>
> **Maya Angelou**

How do you shine? Think about all the ways in which you already shine your light in the world and then add a few more for good measure!

I shine a light in the world by...

Week 3 **Wisdom**

Day 19
Affirmation

This is a simple exercise today and designed for self-love and appreciation.

All you need to do is complete these two statements:

I am here to...
The goodness of me is...

Then say this affirmation to yourself three times:

'There is a place and
   a purpose for everything
under the sun,
      including me.'

I am here to...

The goodness of me is...

Week 3 Wisdom

Day 20
Daydreaming

Today is an opportunity for some play and fun. We have been forensically analyzing the question of purpose for some time now.

Today, we are going to switch gears and give you a chance to let it all go, as you play with the idea of 'purposelessness'.

Within the context of your life, the invitation is to be aimless, like a wandering cloud, at points during your day. This is not about mindless scrolling on social media, but more like a gentle stroll with no devices. Rather than sinking into malaise, this is about a few minutes of looking out of the window and daydreaming.

For one day, give your goals a rest, knowing that they will still be there tomorrow. This is all about creating some space, perhaps enjoying a quiet coffee before the rest of the house wakes up, maybe listening to the birds sing in the woods, perhaps laying back and looking at the clouds.

Whatever resistance your mind has to this, just notice, soften and indulge yourself – you deserve it!

❝❞
Not all those who wander are lost.

J. R. R. Tolkien

Evening reflection

Week 3 **Wisdom**

Day 21
I went to the Master

As the week draws to a close, today is an opportunity to access your higher self and find the thread that pulls it all together. To do this, you may want to begin by returning to the cloud you visited on Day 15, connecting again with the soft, expansive feeling you found there. Then from this soft, open place, write down your responses to the following statement:

I went to the Master and asked: 'Master, how can I be more of me?' And the Master replied…

This is a free-form writing exercise, so let everything come out without censoring it. There's no need for this to be in any kind of polished, coherent order or to be spellchecked. Keep breathing and writing, letting the words flow as they want to, and if you get stuck, go back to the Master and ask again until you feel you have expressed everything you needed to hear today.

Let the words flow as they want to.

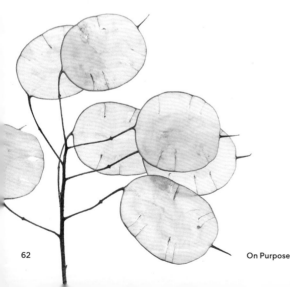

On Purpose

I went to the Master and asked:
'Master, how can I be more of me?'
And the Master replied...

Week 4

North Star

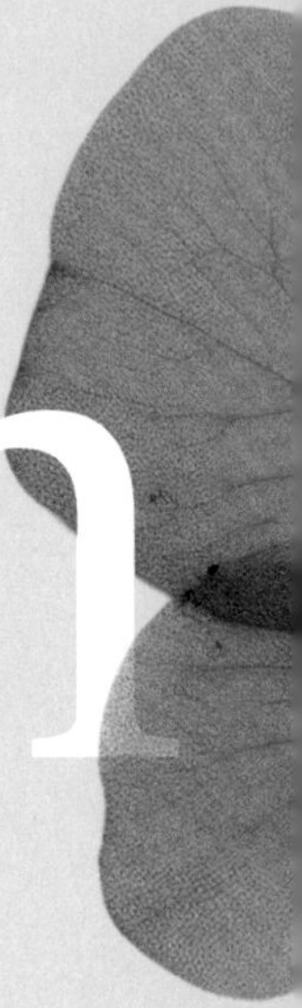

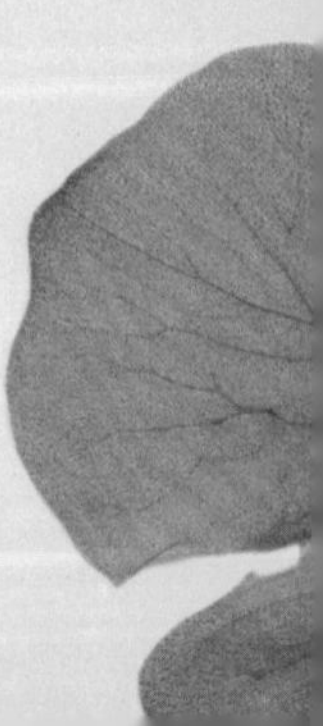

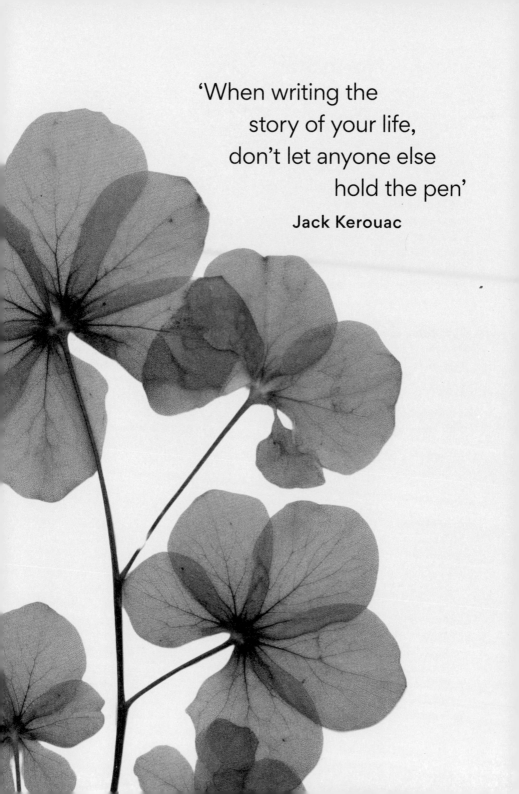

'When writing the
story of your life,
don't let anyone else
hold the pen'

Jack Kerouac

Week 4 North Star

Day 22
To...

The format of purpose is best kept as a simple equation. After all, life is already complicated enough, so you can afford to be gentle with yourself when it comes to your purpose. Soften, loosen, relax. Let it come to you.

To help, here is the structure you are aiming for: 'To + one word that defines your Core Purpose'.

At first you might think this is impossible – how could my purpose possibly be one word?!

When that happens, you could find your mind drawing you back to defining a role or a job description rather than your purpose. This is natural, and so is any confusion you might feel. The beauty of purpose, however, is that it is simple. When you land on it, it will chime inside you, resonating like the pure tone of a crystal singing bowl. You will probably think to yourself, 'Is this it?' and then deep down know, yes, it is.

This is it; it has always been this.

To help you with your reflections, here are some examples:

To Accept
To Affirm
To Align
To Awaken
To Balance
To Bridge
To Build

To Catalyze
To Challenge
To Change
To Cherish
To Connect
To Create
To Crystallize
To Debate
To Develop
To Devote
To Evoke
To Evolve
To Expand

To Forgive
To Grow
To Harmonize
To Heal
To Illuminate
To Initiate
To Inspire
To Lead
To Liberate
To Listen
To Love
To Nourish
To Produce

To Protect
To Relate
To Release
To Resolve
To Respect
To See
To Seek
To Share
To Sparkle
To Trust
To Truth-Tell
To Unite
To Weave

Reflections

Week 4 North Star

Day 23
Purpose is for you and for others

Did you find the words yesterday that encapsulate your purpose? If you did, then one of the ways we can check this is truly 'purpose' is by using the infinity symbol. For purpose to be true and real, it must be for you and for others. Like the infinity symbol, the energy of your purpose nourishes you and nourishes others. Purpose is not one-sided in its expression; it is a reciprocal, mutually beneficial energy that is constantly in equilibrium between giving and receiving.

Additionally, in the same way that you can move from the centre of the ellipse in any direction, so you can also find purpose in any one of an infinite number of different kinds of life. Remember that your purpose is your essence, and the expression of your essence comes in the things you do, the ways in which you contribute, and also in the things you choose not to do.

Affirmation: **'I embrace my purpose which has a positive impact for me and for others.'**

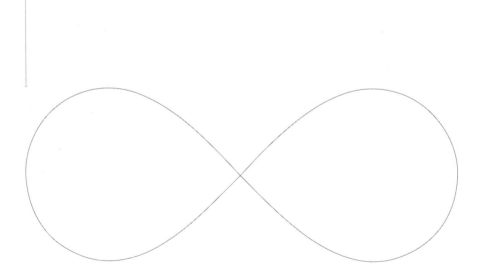

Use this space to explore the ways in which your purpose is both for you and for others, and how it is expressed in the gifts you offer and receive.

North Star

Day 24
Letter from the future

'What we call the beginning is often the end. And to make an end is to make a beginning. The end is where we start from.'

T.S. Eliot, Little Gidding

If you are still seeking the words for your purpose, let's start at the end. Today you are going to write a letter to yourself. Imagine that you are reaching the closing chapter of your life. From this vantage point, write back to your younger self, the you of today. The letter will be filled with admiration, respect, love and kindness. You will also share the wisdom you have learned and, most importantly, the secrets of who you really are, your true nature, and why you are here.

Start the letter:

Dear [your name], and then keep writing...

Space to create

Week 4 North Star

Day 25
Visioning

'When you are dreaming of what is possible for your life, you should know that anything is possible. You may not always feel it or see it, but you never for a single moment lack the capacity to change course. Your life is subject to infinite revision.'

17th Karmapa

We often think of life as linear, but really it's a spiral, sometimes expanding and opening, and other times retracing our steps, contracting and retracting. Visioning is a powerful way to articulate your inner world, so you can begin to realize it in the outer world.

Here's a simple visioning technique:

Think about the ways your purpose could influence the expansion and opening of you in your life. Start in the centre of the page and for the next 6 or 12 months (whatever time frame suits you) begin to draw a spiral that spans this timeframe.

Mark the months on the spiral, and then write a note about what you would love to see month by month. How would the inner expression of your essence, your purpose, manifest in the outer world as you interact with life? What will you be feeling, what will your experience of life be like? To acknowledge the continuum of your life, it can be nice to leave the spiral with an unfinished tail/tale. ☺

Space to create

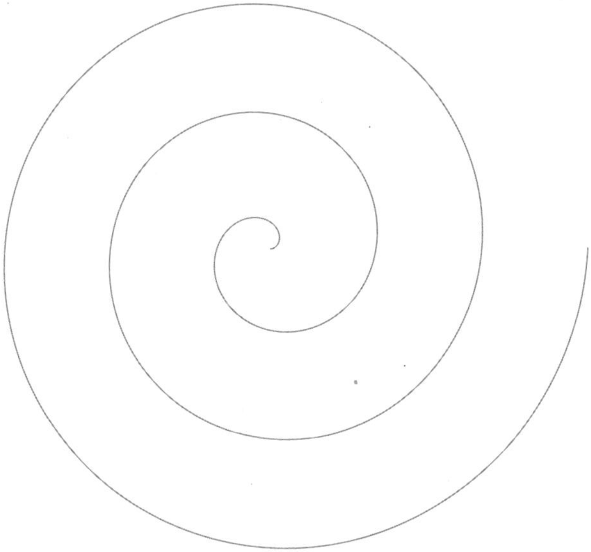

Week 4 **North Star**

Day 26
Be like a tree

Whether you have found your purpose or not, this exercise brings you back to gratitude, which is its own powerful, life-giving energy:

This is a good life because...

_____
_____
_____
_____
_____

I am a good person because...

_____
_____
_____
_____
_____

This is enough because...

_____
_____
_____
_____
_____

Now, on the opposite page, draw a tree – roots, trunk, branches and leaves – and use this to represent all the parts of your life that you feel grateful for.

Who or what:
- Gives you strong roots?
- Guides you to stand tall?
- Encourages you to branch out?
- Nourishes you so that you can flourish?

Space to create your tree

Week 4 North Star

Day 27
Meditation: Step by step

Close your eyes and visualize a door in front of you. Picture the size, shape and colour. Notice the distinctive keyhole. Reach into your pocket and draw out the key to this door. Placing the key in the lock, you notice it fits perfectly. Turning the key, you gently push the door open. It yields easily and, as you open the door, you see a flight of stairs. Picture the stairs exactly as you want to see them. Stepping onto the first step, you count the number of stairs, descending step by step.

At the bottom or the staircase, you see an ornate and beautiful mirror. As you look into this mirror, you see yourself three months into the future. You feel confident, relaxed and strong inside. See yourself exactly as you want to be. Make the picture bright and clear, vivid and colourful.

Breathe deeply as you feel how it feels to be embodying your purpose. Notice if you feel happy, proud, secure, grateful – whatever the feeling is for you, let that feeling grow like the sun's rays gently warming your body. Know that you can feel this way at any time.

Make the return journey up the stairs, bringing the feeling with you, step by step, as you arrive back at the top of the staircase. Standing at the door, you gently pull the door open and arrive back in your body and into your space, just as it is.

On Purpose

Note to self

Week 4 North Star

Anchoring your purpose: How to make a Purpose Board

This is a lovely exercise to spend time doing at the weekend and is a way of embodying your purpose.

You will need:
- Magazines and/or a selection of images that inspire you, such as photographs, illustrations, postcards, quotes.
- Scissors
- Glue
- Large piece of cardboard or foam board

Spend some time finding images that inspire your purpose. Let yourself be guided intuitively to the pictures – they don't all have to 'make sense'.

Ask yourself:
- What is the simplest expression of my purpose?
- What is the highest expression of my purpose?
- What joy does my purpose give me?
- How does living my purpose positively impact others?

Once you have collected your images, use a piece or cardboard or foam board to create your Purpose Board.

If you have connected with a word that reflects your purpose, create your Purpose Board using that word. If you don't have that word yet, use this exercise to find words that resonate with your sense of purpose as you would like it to be. If you are still in doubt, use the word 'peace'. Peace will lead you to your purpose in time.

As we draw to the end of this process, it is of course, just the beginning! You have been on a deep reflective journey of inner work, and you will be changed as a result of this. As you integrate all of your discoveries and perhaps grapple with some new or unanswered questions, remember that you belong here, at this point in time,

in the infinite dance of life.

About Danielle

Danielle North is the founder of Pause Global, a talent development consultancy that takes a unique but simple approach: if you're going to perform in a world that's speeding up, sometimes you need to slow down.

Partnering with HR teams around the world, Pause addresses the challenges people face, from stress management and burnout to career performance and personal transformation. Danielle's books include *Pause, Pause Every Day, Sleep Meditations* and *Morning Meditations*.

www.pauseglobal.com

Information:
First published:
Inner Work Project, 2024
Text copyright ©
Danielle North 2024

By kind permission:

p.12 Ashworth, Donna.
(2022) *I Wish I Knew*.
Edinburgh: Black and White
Publishing

Graphic Design:
Supafrank

Printed in the UK by Pureprint

Discover more workbooks
to put your good intentions
into daily practice.

www.innerworkproject.com